CW00926463

Doodled
CATS

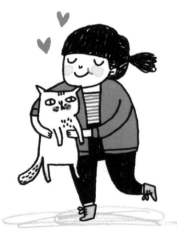

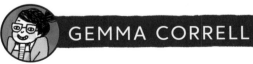

GEMMA CORRELL

Brimming with creative inspiration, how-to projects, and useful information to enrich your everyday life, Quarto Knows is a favorite destination for those pursuing their interests and passions. Visit our site and dig deeper with our books into your area of interest: Quarto Creates, Quarto Cooks, Quarto Homes, Quarto Lives, Quarto Drives, Quarto Explores, Quarto Gifts, or Quarto Kids.

© 2018 Quarto Publishing Group USA Inc.
Artwork and font © 2015 Gemma Correll

First Published in 2015 by Walter Foster Publishing, an imprint of The Quarto Group.
6 Orchard Road, Suite 100, Lake Forest, CA 92630, USA.
T (949) 380-7510 F (949) 380-7575 www.QuartoKnows.com

All rights reserved. No part of this book may be reproduced in any form without written permission of the copyright owners. All images in this book have been reproduced with the knowledge and prior consent of the artists concerned, and no responsibility is accepted by producer, publisher, or printer for any infringement of copyright or otherwise, arising from the contents of this publication. Every effort has been made to ensure that credits accurately comply with information supplied. We apologize for any inaccuracies that may have occurred and will resolve inaccurate or missing information in a subsequent reprinting of the book.

Walter Foster Publishing titles are also available at discount for retail, wholesale, promotional, and bulk purchase. For details, contact the Special Sales Manager by email at specialsales@quarto.com or by mail at The Quarto Group, Attn: Special Sales Manager, 401 Second Avenue North, Suite 310, Minneapolis, MN 55401 USA.

ISBN: 978-1-63322-653-1

Illustrated and written by Gemma Correll
Select text by Stephanie Carbajal

Printed in China
10 9 8 7 6 5 4 3 2 1

MIX
Paper from responsible sources
FSC
www.fsc.org FSC® C104723

Table of Contents

How to Use This Book

This book is just a guide. Each artist has his or her own style. Using your imagination will make the drawings more unique and special! The fun of doodling comes from not trying too hard. So don't worry about making mistakes or trying to achieve perfection.

Here are some tips to help you get the most of this doodling book.

DOODLE PROMPTS

The prompts in this book are designed to get your creative juices flowing—and your pen and pencil moving! Don't think too much about the prompts; just start drawing and see where your imagination takes you. There's no such thing as a mistake in doodling!

STEP-BY-STEP EXERCISES

Following the step-by-step exercises is fun and easy! The red lines show you the next step. The black lines are the steps you've already completed.

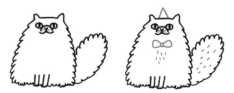

SUPPLIES

Doodling doesn't require any special tools or materials. You can draw with anything you like! Here are a few of my favorite drawing tools.

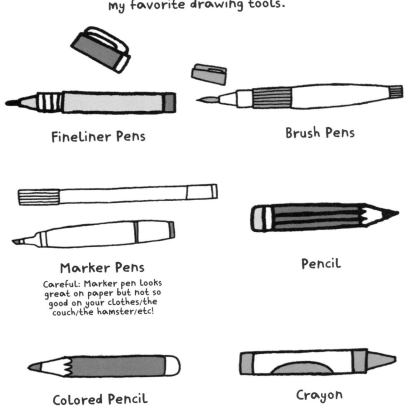

Fineliner Pens

Brush Pens

Marker Pens

Careful: Marker pen looks great on paper but not so good on your clothes/the couch/the hamster/etc!

Pencil

Colored Pencil

Crayon

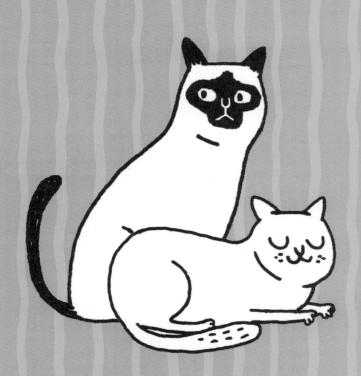

Part 1

ALL
ABOUT
CATS

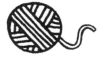

DRAW OR PASTE A PICTURE OF YOUR CAT IN THE FRAME.

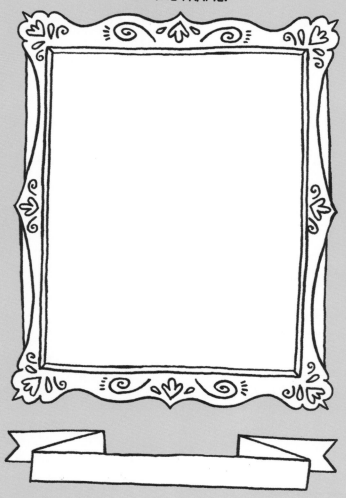

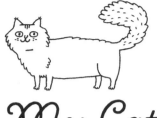

My Cat

Favorite Game: chase liv up the stairs.

Favorite place to sleep: on the dining room chair.

Favorite toy: straw

Favorite snack or treat: dreumies

Favorite way to be naughty: bite feet.

20 Signs you're a CAT Person

1   You celebrate your cat's birthday.

2   Your phone is full of photos of your cat—not your friends and loved ones.

3   You have been known to call your cats "my children."

4   You are perpetually covered in cat fur.

5   You send holiday cards cosigned (with a paw print, of course!) by your cat.

6   You eat budget tuna, while your pampered cat feasts on deluxe, organic salmon.

7   You keep all of your cardboard boxes for kitty to play in.

8   You have a gold card at the pet store.

9   Your entire living room is occupied by a giant cat tree.

10 Your pockets are full of kitty treats.

11 You talk to your cats when nobody else is around.

12 You talk to your cats when other people are around...you just don't care.

13 Your cat has her own website and Facebook page.

14 Your email address is catperson@ilovecats.com.

15 Your shelves are full of cat ornaments, books about cats, photos of cats, and random cat toys.

16 At any given moment, you know that there are at least 11 cat toys under the couch.

17 Cat hair in your food is just extra fiber, right?

18 You'd rather spend a night on the couch with your cats than go out on the town.

19 You're not actually sure how many cats you own, but it's at least five.

20 You're not a "Crazy Cat Person"—You're a "Feline Enthusiast."

A Day in the Life

Eating, sleeping, and ruling the world...our spoiled fur babies are truly livin' the life.

7:30 AM   Yowl repeatedly outside Human's door until Human gets out of bed

8 AM   Breakfast—scatter a few pieces of food on the floor to save for later

10 AM   Nap on the sofa...

11 AM   .....

12 PM   .....

1 PM   Window Watch Patrol—hiss at the neighbor's dog

3 PM   Shred toilet paper roll

4 PM   Nap on kitchen chair...

5 PM	.....
6 PM	.....
6:30 PM	Deign to be petted and brushed by Human
8 PM	Nap on Human's lap
9 PM	.....
10 PM	Chase paper clip around the house
11 PM	Tear up and down the hallways to ward off evil spirits
12 AM	Nap until duty calls again...

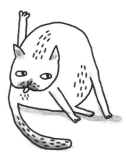

Cat-toids

Felines are both universally loved and abhorred—
by a small, insignificant, insane segment of the
human population—and are one of earth's
most fascinating creatures. Here are just
a few reasons why...

 Fact: Your kitty's nose has a unique ridged pattern—like a human fingerprint!

Fact: Felines spend nearly a third of their waking hours grooming themselves.

 Fact: Cats have more than 20 muscles that control their ears.

Fact: A kitty can jump up to five times its length.

Fact: A group of cats is called a "clowder."

Fact: A group of kittens is called a "kindle."

Fact: Cats can make about 100 different sounds.

Fact: Your favorite furry friend may or may not be, but most likely is, plotting your demise.

Fact: Kitties conserve energy by sleeping for an average of 13 to 14 hours.

 Fact: More than 40 percent of cats are right-pawed or left-pawed...leaving the rest ambidextrous!

Fact: In ancient Egypt, all cats were revered as sacred, helpful, and lucky—something the species has never forgotten.

 Fact: A cat's brain, though small, is more complex than a dog's.

Fact: Kitties only meow to communicate with humans, not with other cats!

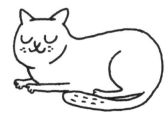

Cattitude

From sweet to sassy, kitties are masters of expressing themselves, be it affection or disdain. Our feline friends have attitude... and they're not afraid to show it!

Have you no sense of dignity, Malcolm?

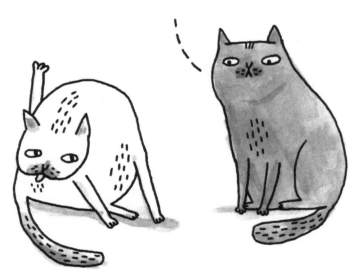

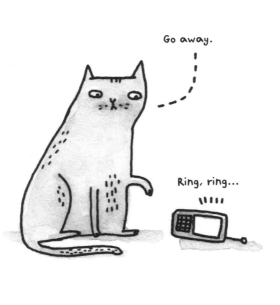

17

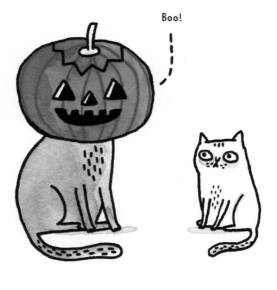

18

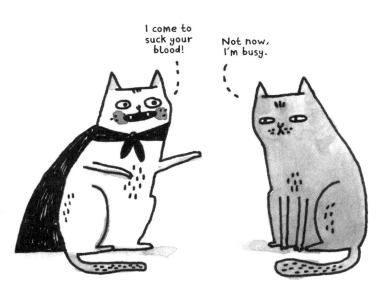

You are beautiful, but you have an ugly soul.

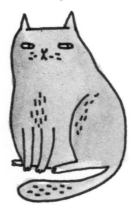

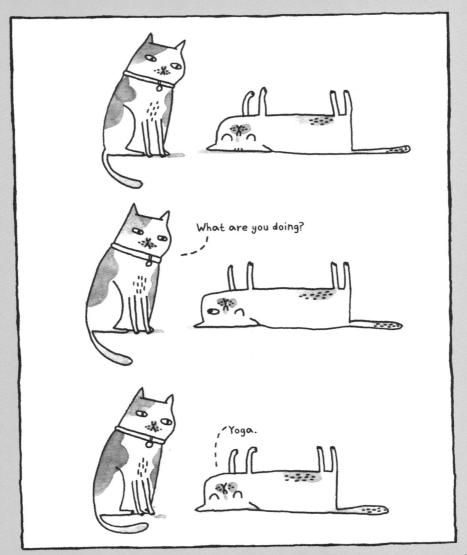

21

Doodled Cat Faces

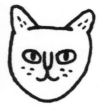 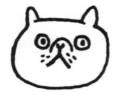 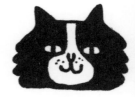

Some cats have long faces.
Others have round or square faces.

  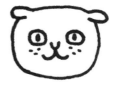

Some cats have big ears.
Some cats have little ears, or even folded ears.

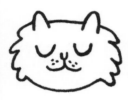  

Some cats are very fluffy.

Some cats have squishy noses.

Cats have all sorts of different
facial markings.

 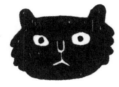 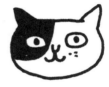

Some cats have very simple markings.

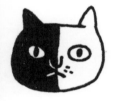 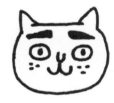 

Some cats have unusual markings.

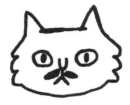  

Some cats have mustaches.

Cat-Spressions

Cats make all kinds of expressions, and they're not shy about letting you know how they feel! Below are some common feline facial expressions.

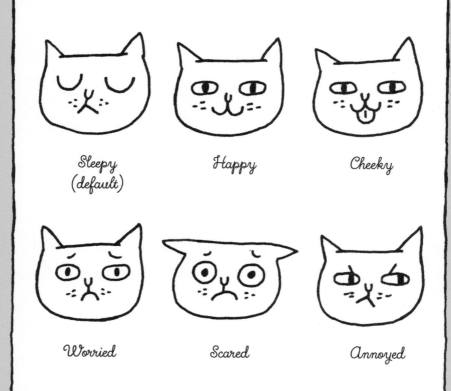

Sleepy
(default)

Happy

Cheeky

Worried

Scared

Annoyed

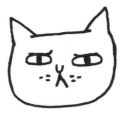

Suspicious

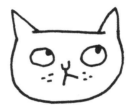

Thoughtful

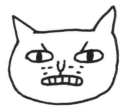

Angry

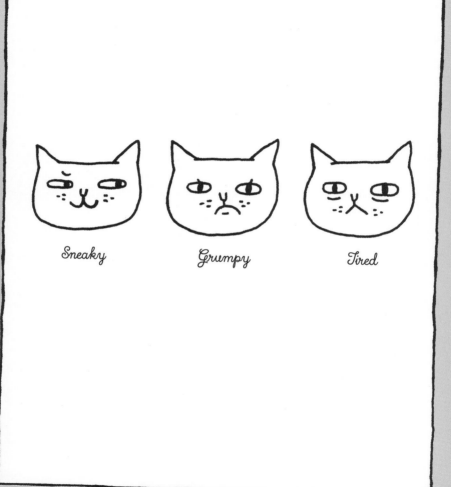

Sneaky   Grumpy   Tired

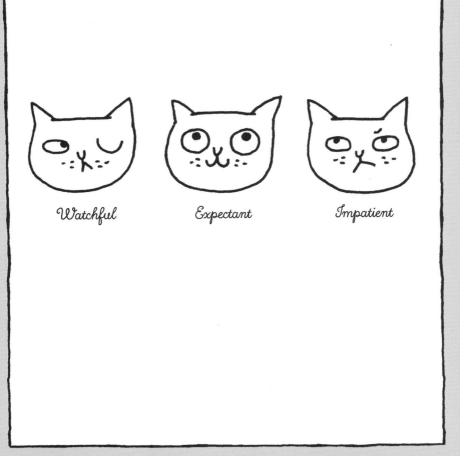

Watchful   Expectant   Impatient

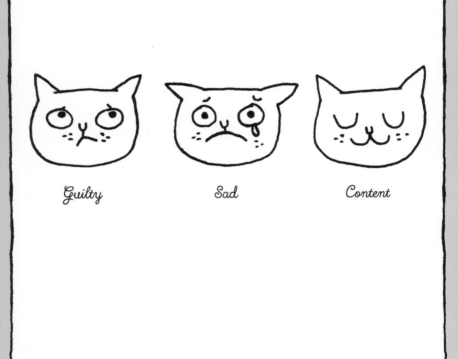

Guilty   Sad   Content

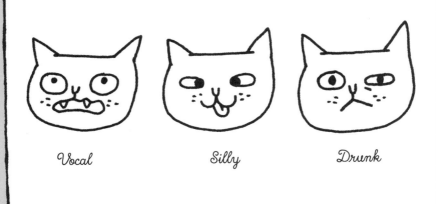

Vocal   Silly   Drunk

Doodled Cats

Cats come in all different varieties—
some have long hair, some have short hair,
and some have no hair.

SHORTHAIR CATS

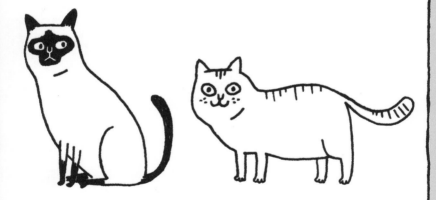

Siamese   *American Shorthair*

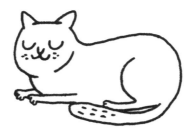

Russian Blue

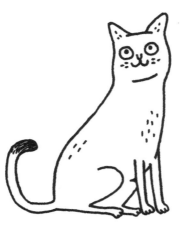

Abyssinian

LONGHAIR CATS

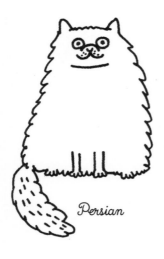

Persian

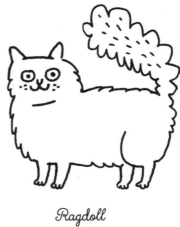

Ragdoll

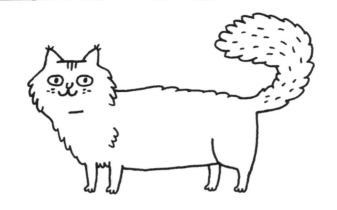

Maine Coon

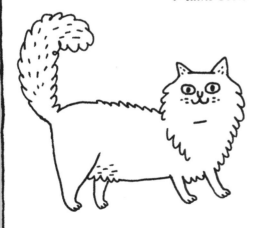

Norwegian Forest Cat

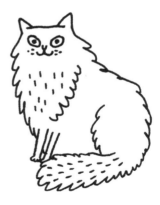

Turkish Angora

UNUSUAL CATS

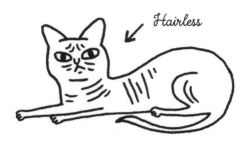

Hairless

Sphynx

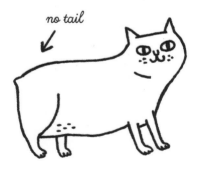

no tail

Manx

folded ears

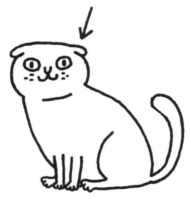

Scottish Fold

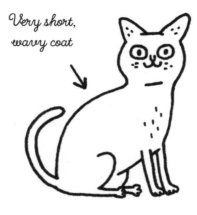

Very short, wavy coat

Devon Rex

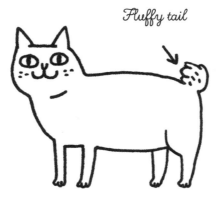

Fluffy tail

Japanese Bobtail

Kitty kingdoms

What does your feline friend need to feel like King (or Queen) of the World at home? Here's a checklist to make sure Fluffy has nothing but the best.

O   Basket of expensive toys

O   Cardboard box

O   Ball of tinfoil

O   Window seat for people watching

O   Big-screen TV

O   Scratching post

O   Catnip...every hour on the hour

O   Lifetime supply of Fancy Feast®

O   Extensive hunting grounds

O   Multiple napping spots

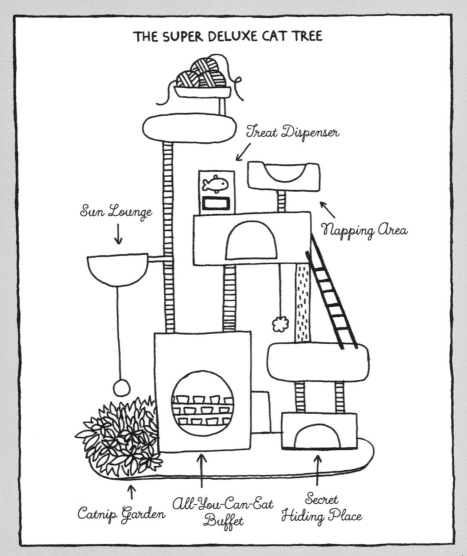

THE SUPER DELUXE CAT TREE

Treat Dispenser

Sun Lounge

Napping Area

Catnip Garden

All-You-Can-Eat Buffet

Secret Hiding Place

45

What's in a Name?

Stumped on what to name your next furry friend? Check out these suggestions for inspiration. Then add your own ideas to the list!

Hubris (hyoo-bris)
noun: a great or foolish amount of pride or confidence

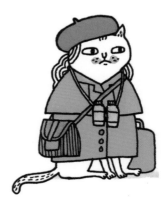

Gouda
Mmmm, cheese...

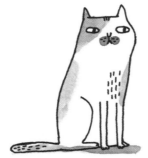

Nutmeg
After your favorite spice

Houdini
For the cleverest of cats

Armani
For the fashion lover

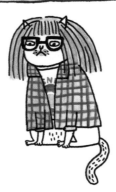

Your Majesty
No explanation needed

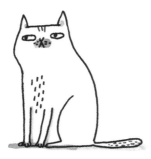

Chianti
Because what more do you need on a Friday night?

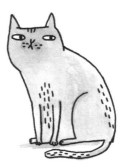

Egypt
To pay homage to your feline's ancestral roots

Sir Naps-a-lot
Because...well...you know

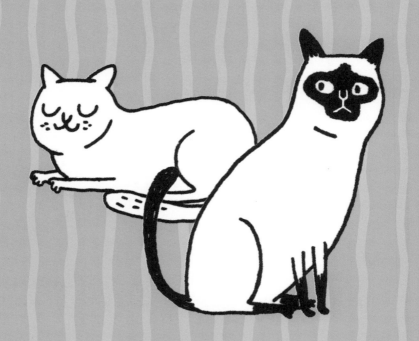

Part 2

DOODLED
CATS
STEP
BY
STEP

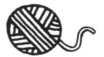

Draw A Kitty

1. Start with the face and ears...

Draw in this direction. Try and do it in one continuous line.

2. Next add the tail...

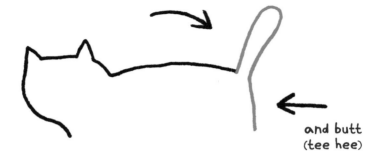

and butt
(tee hee)

3. Give the poor cat some legs already!

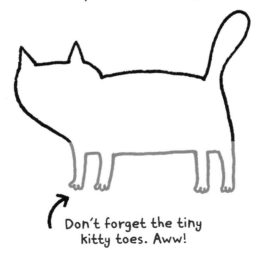

Don't forget the tiny
kitty toes. Aww!

51

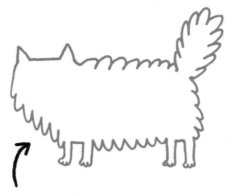

Follow the same basic outline
but make your line squiggly for
a fluffy cat.

4. Let's draw the face now.
Try out some different expressions.

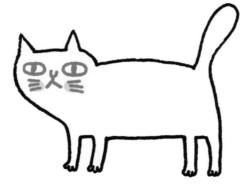

5. Add some essential details.

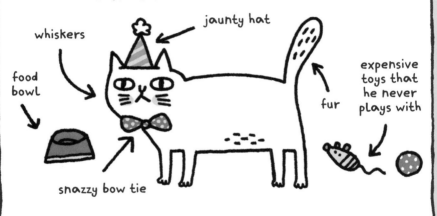

whiskers

jaunty hat

food bowl

expensive toys that he never plays with

fur

snazzy bow tie

53

Draw a Cozy
Curled-Up Kitty

1. Start by drawing the ears.

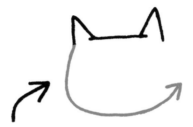

2. Then draw a curve for the head.
   Stop at the bottom right corner.

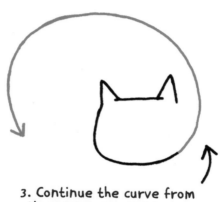

3. Continue the curve from the neck in a semicircle.

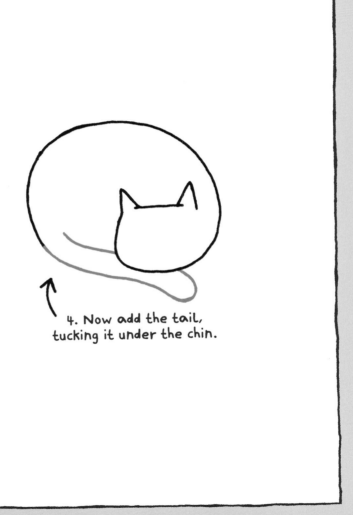

4. Now add the tail, tucking it under the chin.

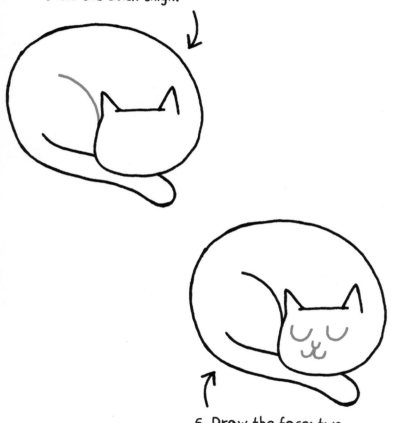

5. Add a little curve to show the back thigh.

6. Draw the face: two semicircles for the closed eyes, a nose, and a mouth.

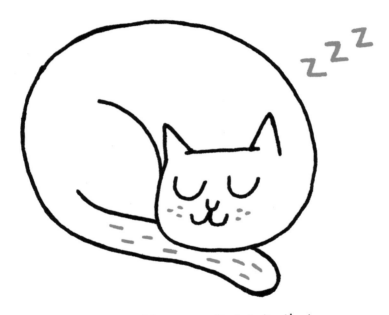

7. Lastly, add any small details that you like—whiskers, fur, stripes, etc.

Draw a Kitty Sitting Pretty

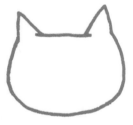

1. Draw the head first.

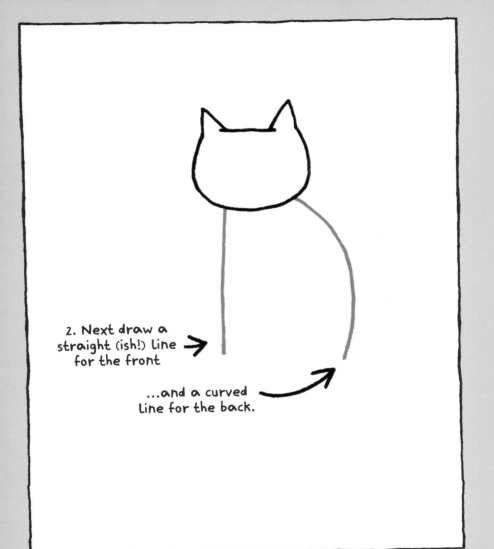

2. Next draw a straight (ish!) line for the front

...and a curved line for the back.

3. Add paws and the other front Leg.

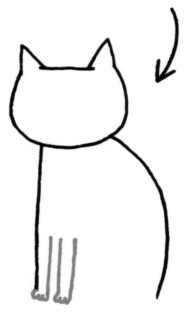

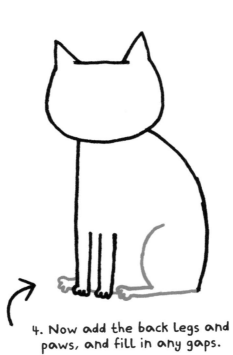

4. Now add the back legs and paws, and fill in any gaps.

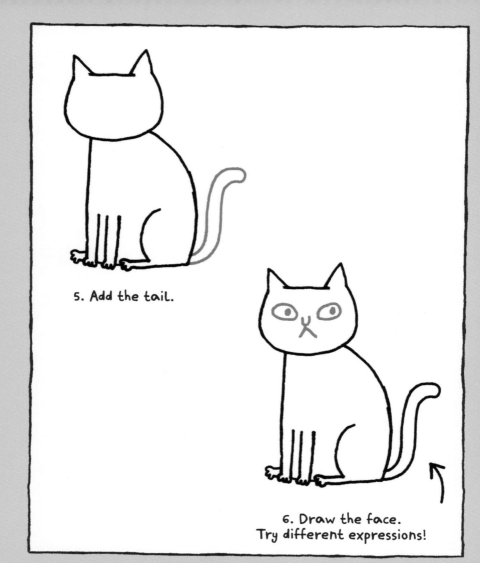

5. Add the tail.

6. Draw the face.
Try different expressions!

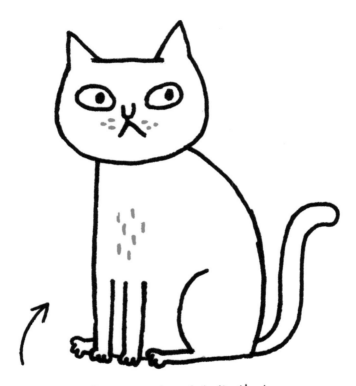

7. Doodle any extra details that you feel like adding...and you're finished!

Draw a Str-E-E-E-tching Kitty

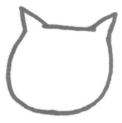

1. Draw the head.

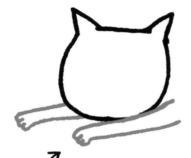

2. Then the two front
   legs and paws.

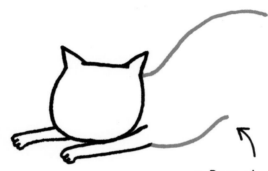

3. Draw two lines curving upward. Get that kittybutt in the air!

Leave a gap for the tail.

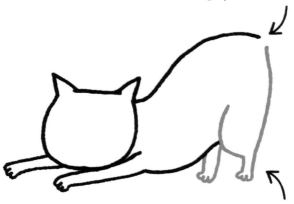

4. Next draw the back legs
and paws like this.

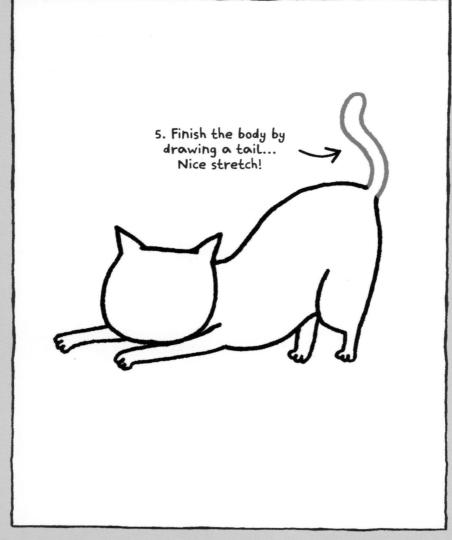

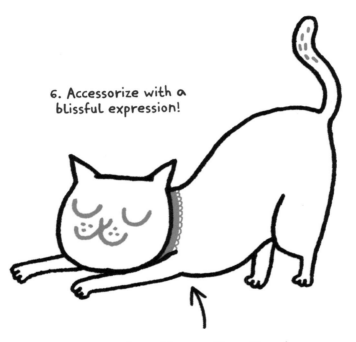

6. Accessorize with a blissful expression!

Maybe add a pretty collar too.

Draw a Perky Fluffy Persian

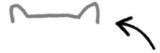

1. Draw the ears. Persian cats have smaller, more rounded ears.

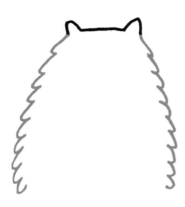

2. Draw the sides. Make them big and fluffy!

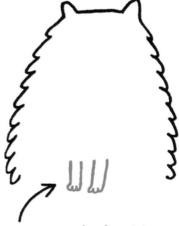

3. Add the front legs and the paws.

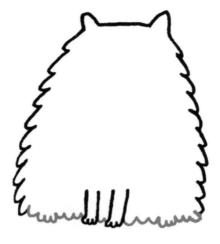

4. Then draw the bottom.
(The back paws are in there
somewhere!)

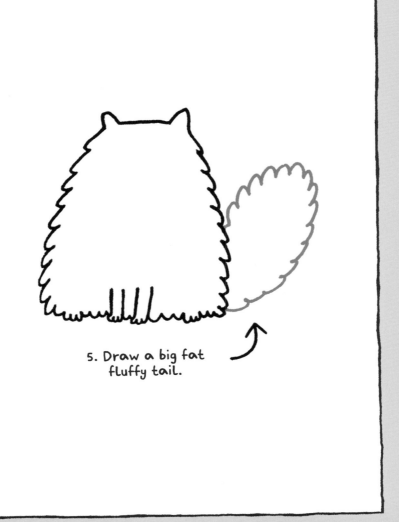

5. Draw a big fat
fluffy tail.

Persian cats have adorably squishy faces.

6. Start by drawing the eyes, and then add a semicircle right below them.

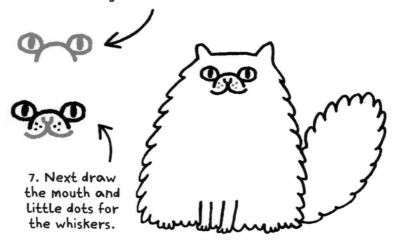

7. Next draw the mouth and little dots for the whiskers.

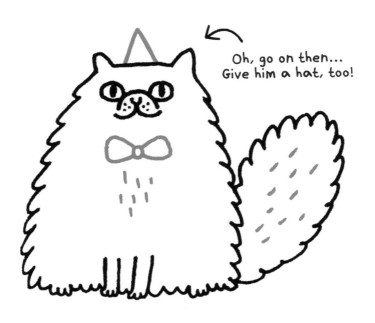

Oh, go on then...
Give him a hat, too!

8. Doodle some lines to represent fur—
and a little bow tie for extra fanciness!

Draw a Super Sphynx

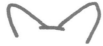

1. Start by drawing the ears. Sphynx ears are a little bigger than those of other cats.

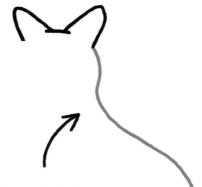

2. Starting at the base of the right ear, draw a curved line that curls all the way around at the bottom (this is the tail).

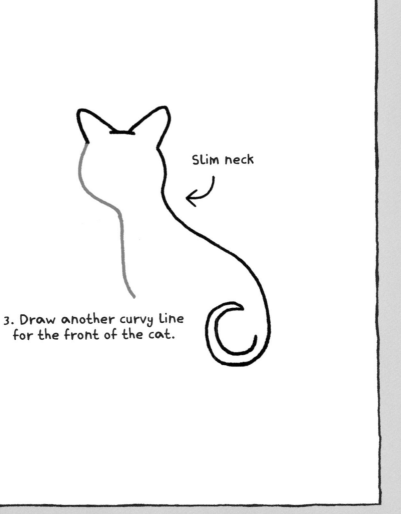

Slim neck

3. Draw another curvy line for the front of the cat.

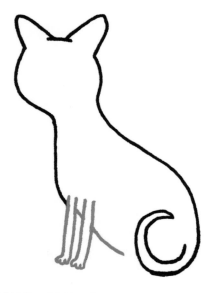

4. Next add the front legs and belly.

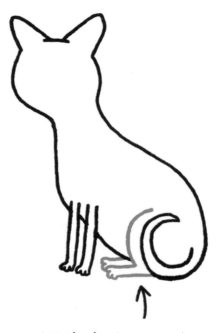

5. Add the back legs and paws.

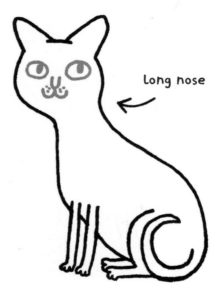

Long nose

6. Draw the face.

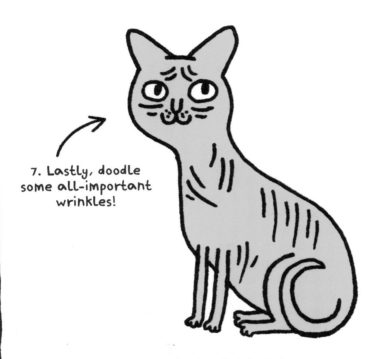

7. Lastly, doodle some all-important wrinkles!

Well done! You've finished drawing your sweet sphynx cat!

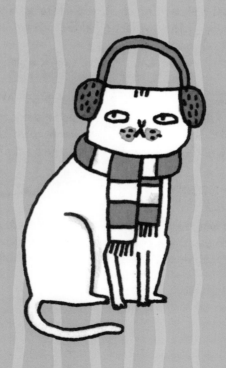

Part 3
IT'S A CAT'S WORLD

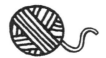

Cats in Hats

Some cats were born to be stars!

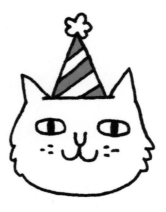

Party Hat

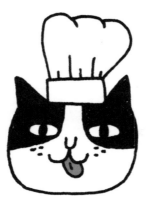

Chef's Hat

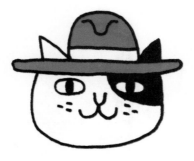

Fedora

Top Hat

Beanie

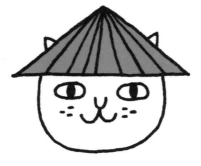

Nón Lá

Doodle hats on these kitty heads...

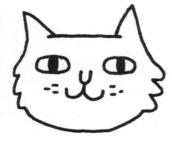

Tam O'Shanter

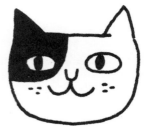

Beret

Crown

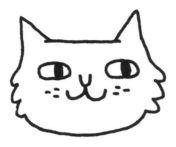

Cowboy Hat

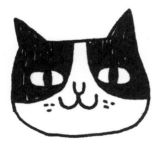

Baseball Cap

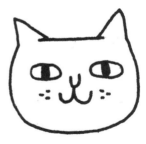

Wizard's Hat

Funky Feline Fur

You've seen tabby cats and tortoiseshell cats, but have you ever seen a polka-dot cat?

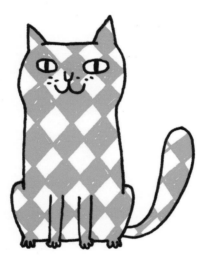

Harlequin

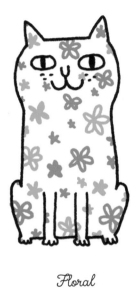

Floral

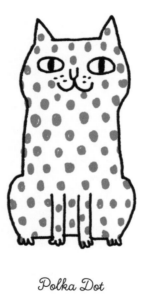

Polka Dot

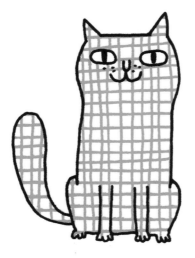

Plaid

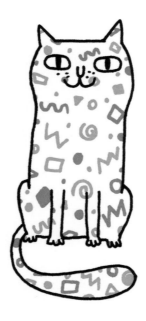

Abstract

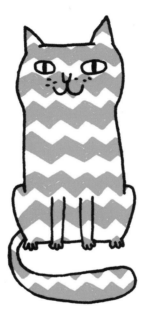

Zigzag

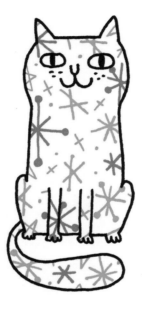

Atomic

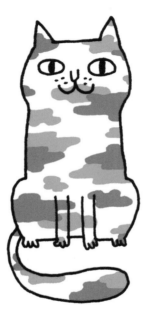

Camo

Anthropomorphic Cats

Cats don't work. Humans work to buy things for cats—that's just the way it is. But imagine if cats did have jobs... These cats have been anthropomorphized (that's fancy talk for "attributing human characteristics to animals"). To draw an anthropomorphic cat, just imagine you're drawing a person, but with a cat's head, tail, and paws.

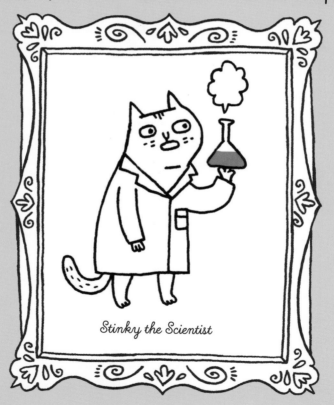

Stinky the Scientist

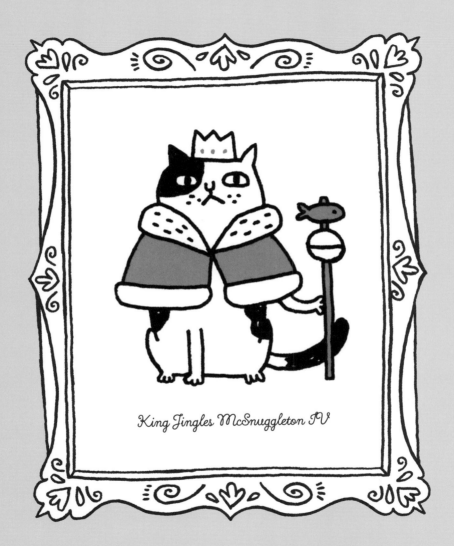

King Jingles McSnuggleton IV

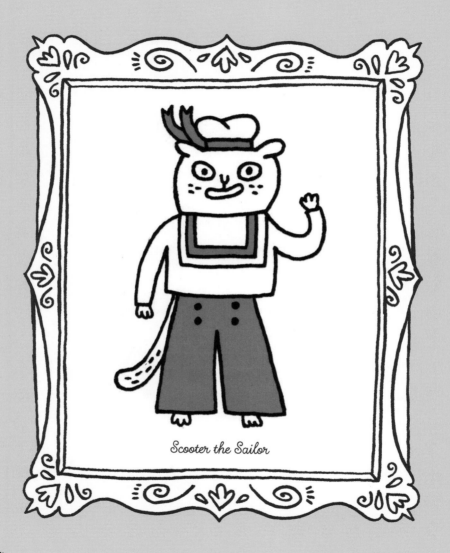

Scooter the Sailor

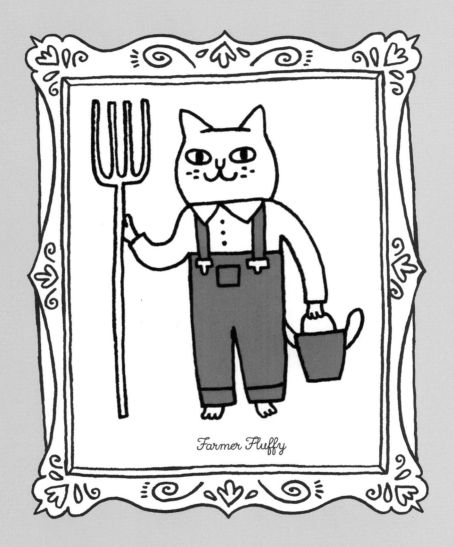

Farmer Fluffy

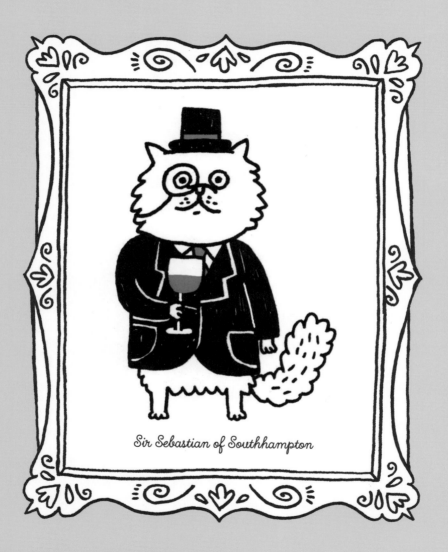

Sir Sebastian of Southhampton

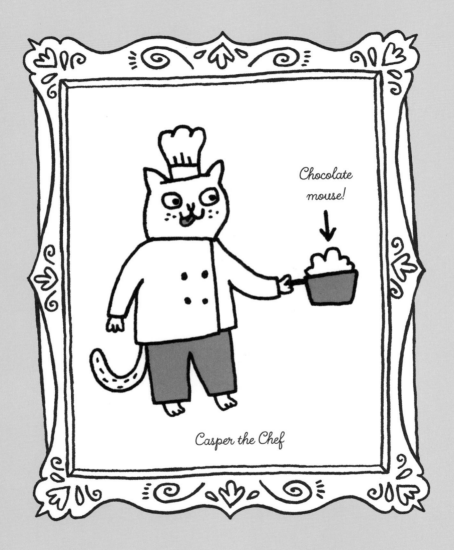

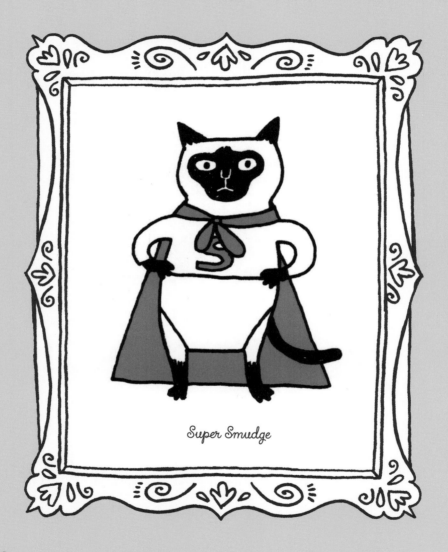

Super Smudge

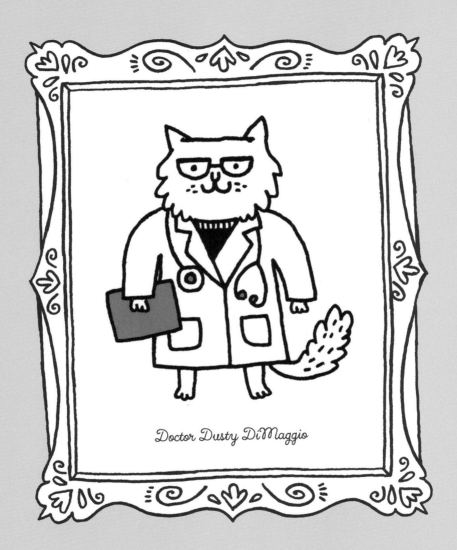

Doctor Dusty DiMaggio

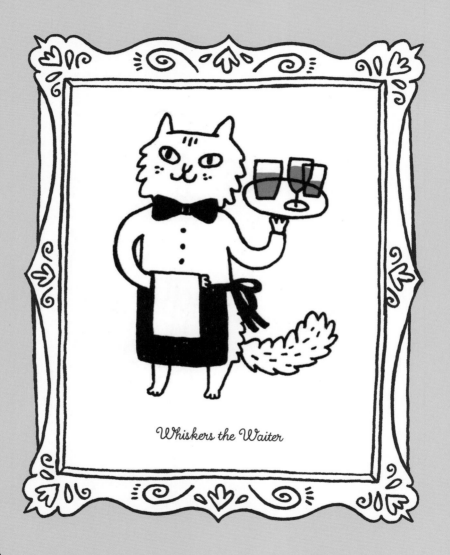

Whiskers the Waiter

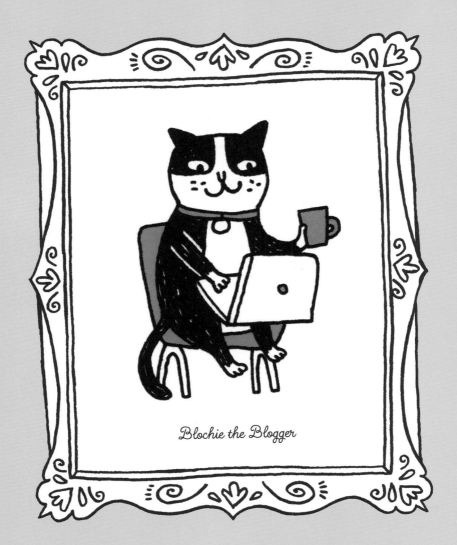

Blochie the Blogger

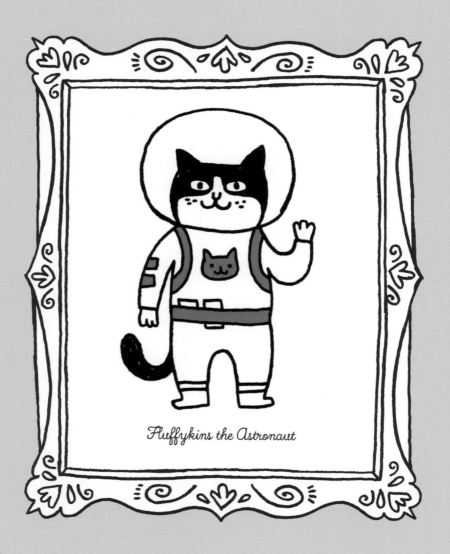

Fluffykins the Astronaut

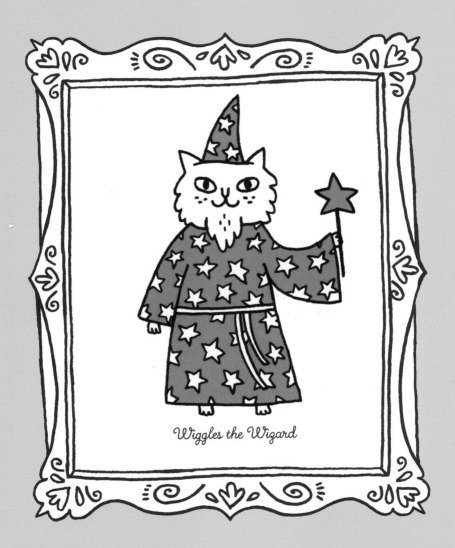

Wiggles the Wizard

Draw an Anthropomorphic Cat

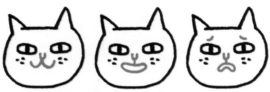

1. Start by drawing the head, just like you would for a "real" cat. Experiment with different facial expressions.

2. Now draw the body, upright like a person (but cuter).

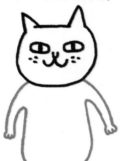

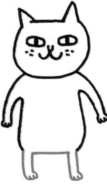

3. Next draw the legs and paws. You might also like to try adding little shoes or booties.

4. Draw a tail if you want to.

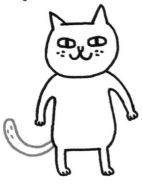

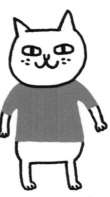

5. Then give him some clothes.

Try out different outfits for your awesome anthropomorphic animal!

Design a T-shirt for your kitty.

Or doodle some cute rosy cheeks!

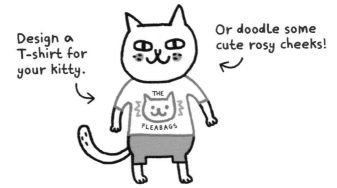

Fashionable Furballs

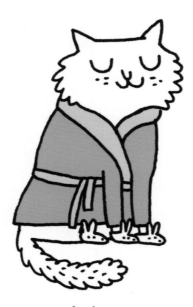

The Homebody

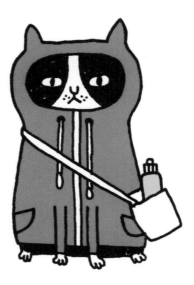

The Adventurer

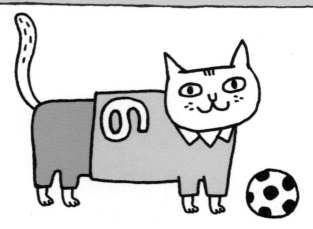

The Sporty

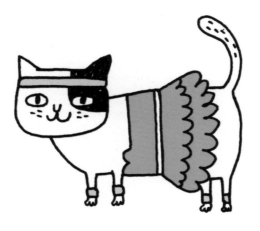

The Exercise Fanatic

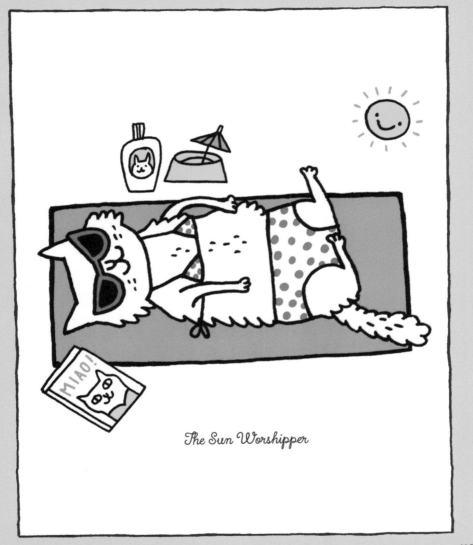

The Sun Worshipper

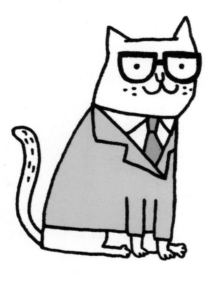

The Smarty Pants

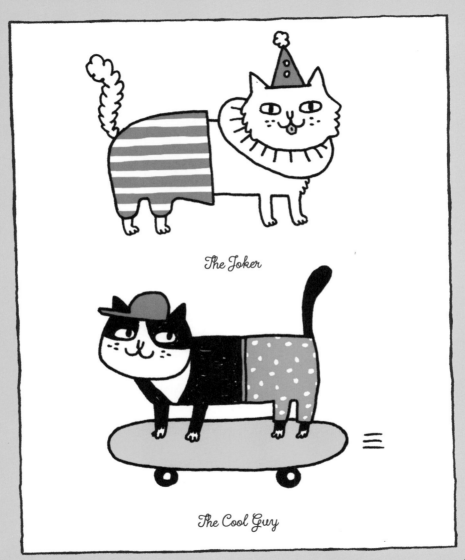

The Joker

The Cool Guy

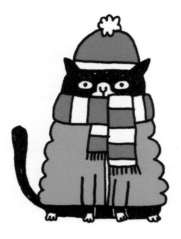

The Snuggler

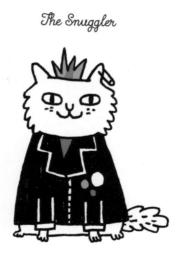

The Punk

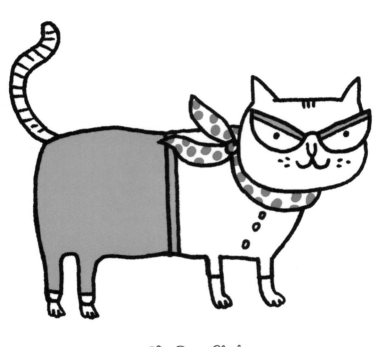

The Retro Chick

Cats Doing Tricks

Unlike their canine counterparts, cats can be difficult to train. This isn't because they can't perform. They simply won't. Go ahead and try it.

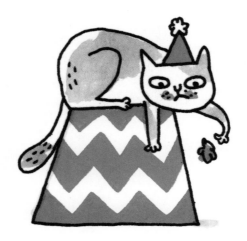

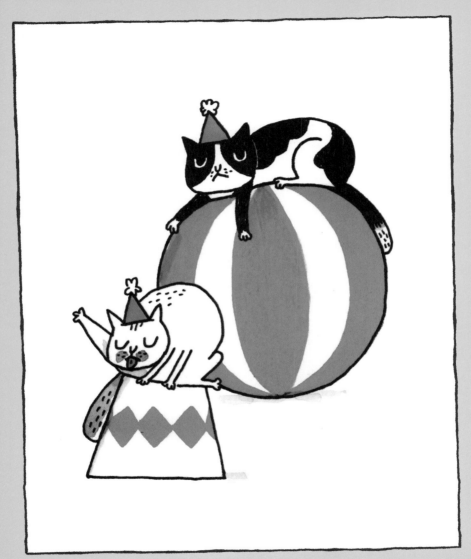

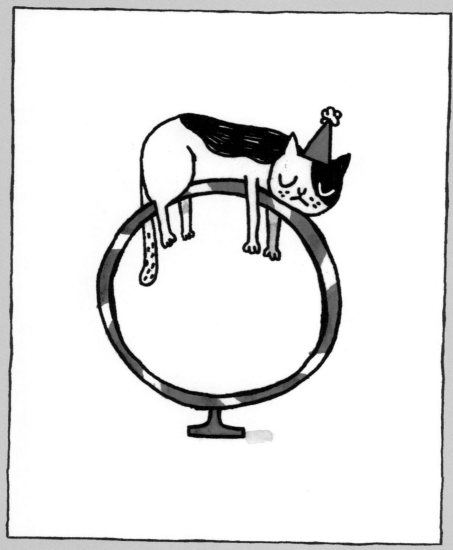

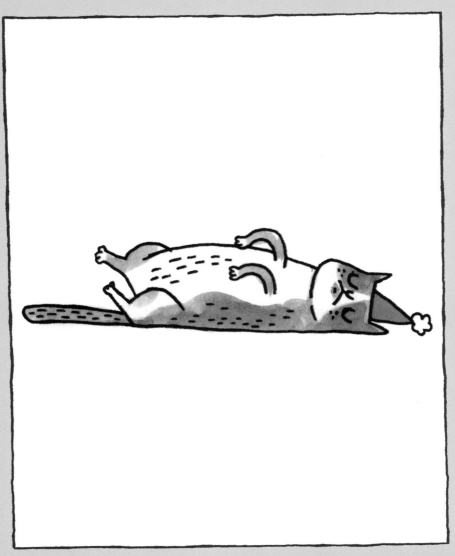

Playtime!

Here are some favorite cat toys.

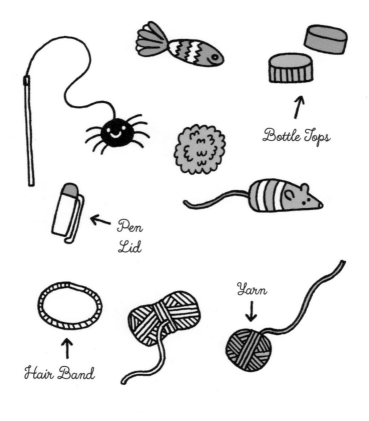

Bottle Tops

Pen Lid

Hair Band

Yarn

It's no secret that cats love squeezing into boxes.
Even if they don't really fit!

APPLES

I think I might be stuck.

Draw your cat in this box.

Kitties on Vacation

These cats are all ready to go on their travels.
Where do they think they are going?

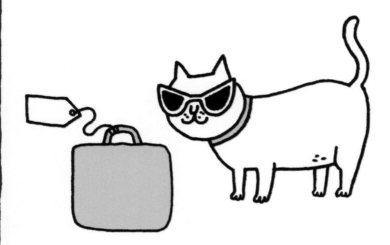

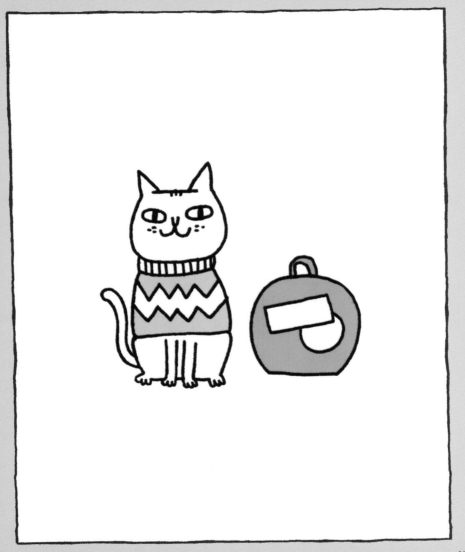

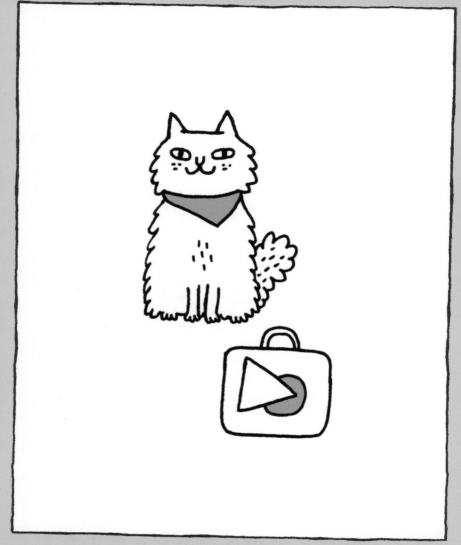

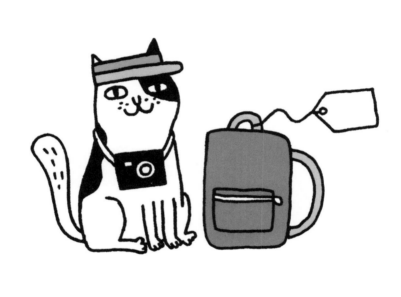

Cats & Dogs

Lovers or haters? You decide!

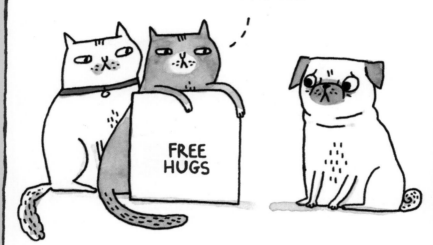

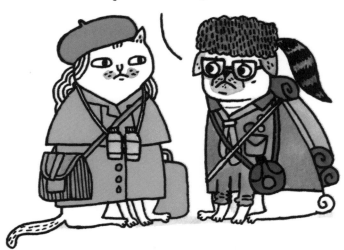

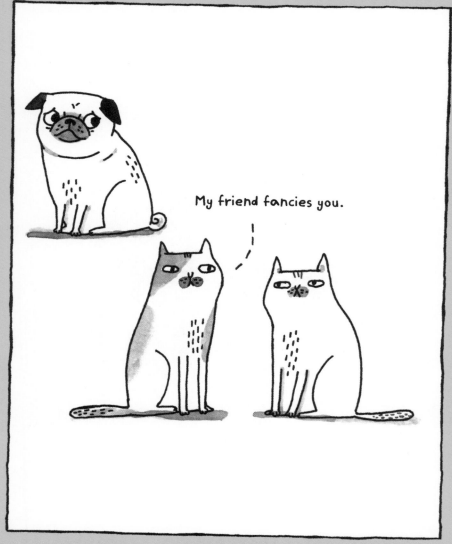

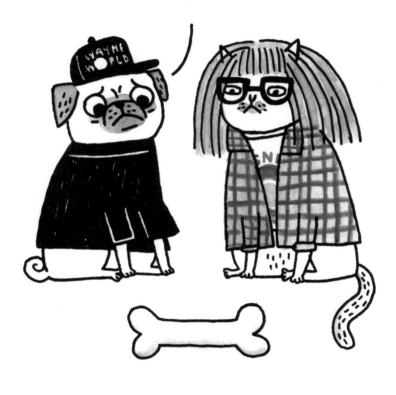

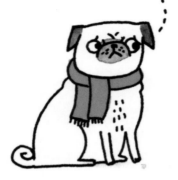
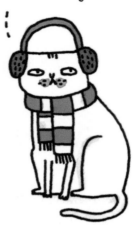
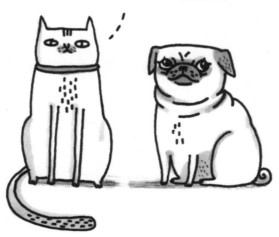

You, sir, are a
bumbling idiot.

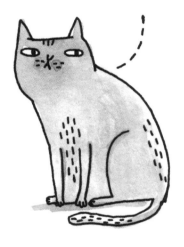
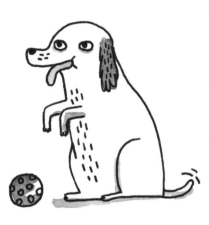

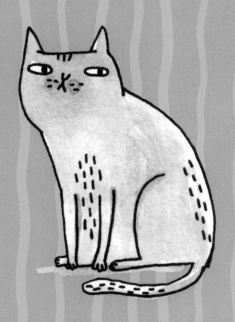

Part 4

CAT
DOODLE
TEMPLATES

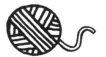

Doodle fur-tastic designs onto these pretty kitties.
Then add kitty treats, toys, food, etc.

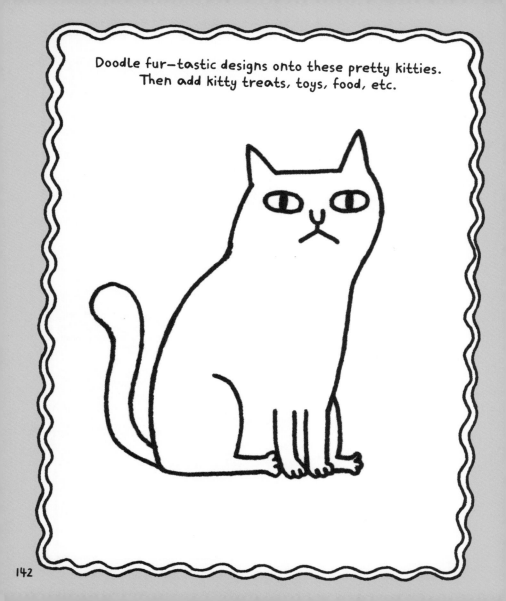

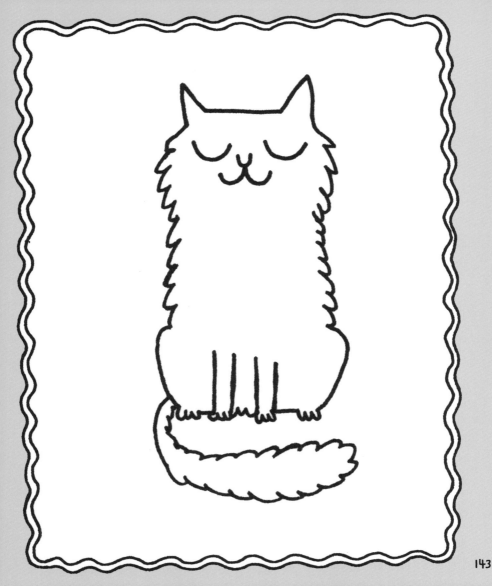

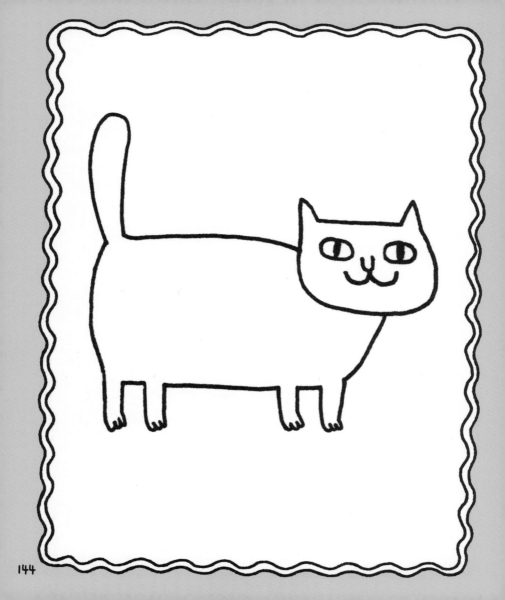

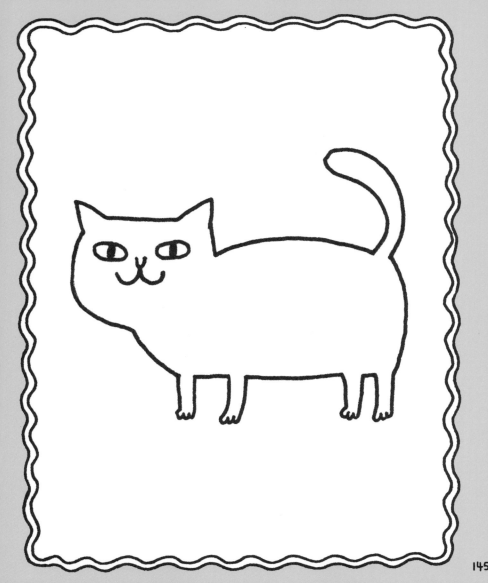

145

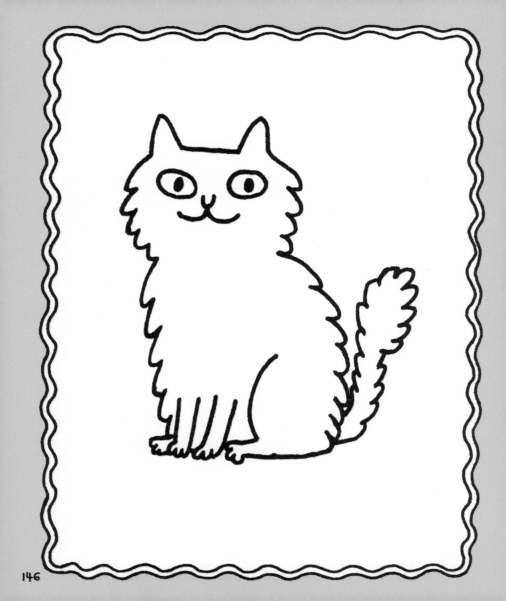

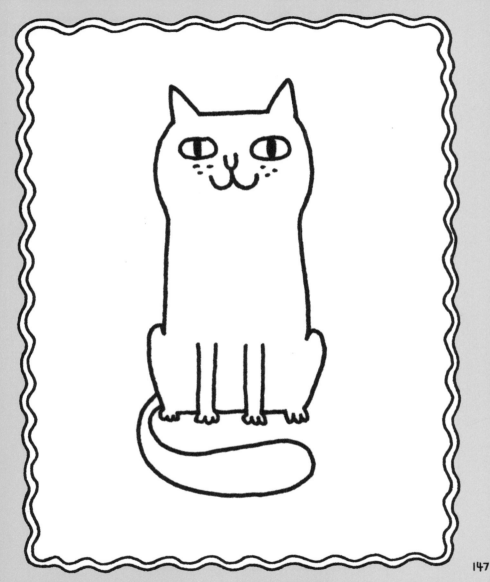

Design some fabulous outfits for these kitties.

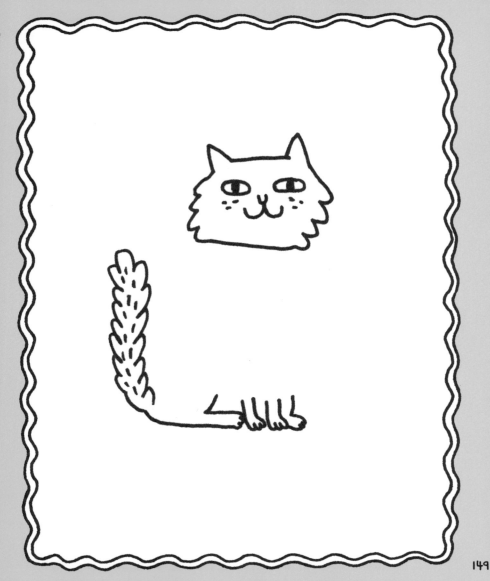

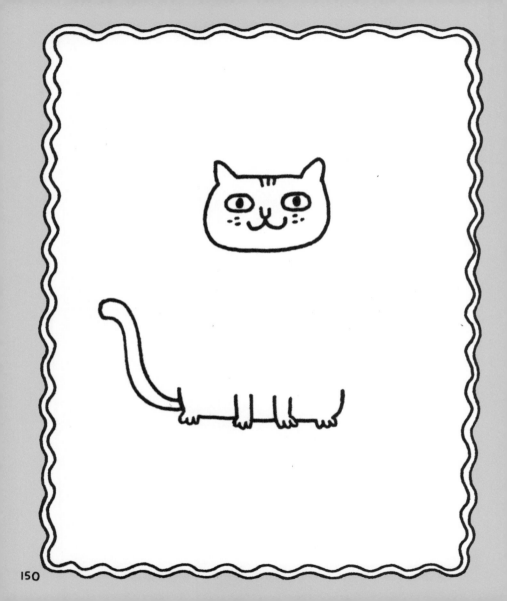

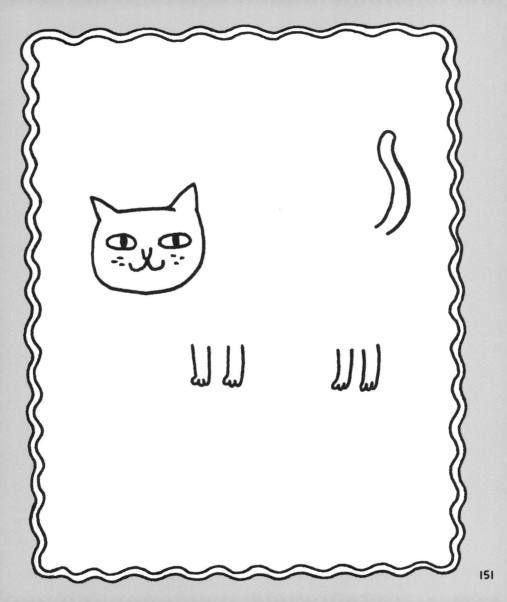

Make a Doodled Mug

Here's what you'll need:

White
Ceramic
Mug

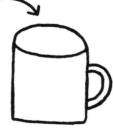

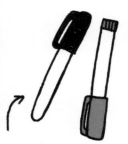
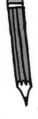

Pencil
(optional)

Ceramic paint pens or
permanent markers
(any colors)

Wet Wipes

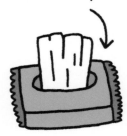

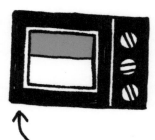

An oven, preset to
350*f / 180*c (optional)

1. Decide what you're going to draw on the mug.

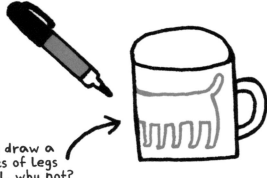

I'm going to draw a cat with lots of legs because...well, why not?

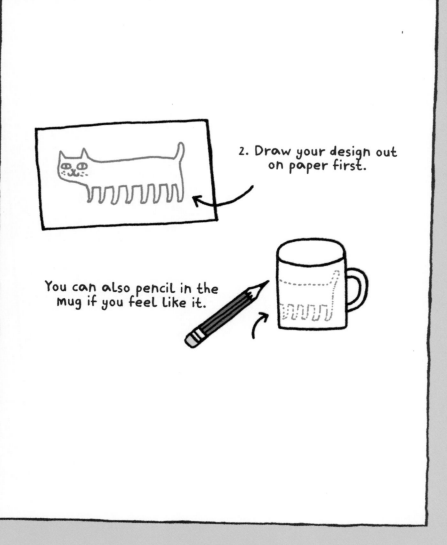

2. Draw your design out on paper first.

You can also pencil in the mug if you feel like it.

3. Start drawing your
design on the mug.

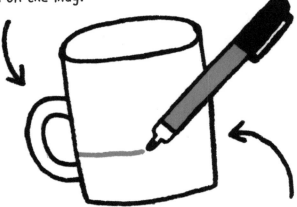

Start on the opposite side of
your drawing hand so that you
don't smudge your artwork as
you go around the mug.

Don't worry if you make a mistake—just wipe it clean with a wet wipe while the ink is still wet. (Make sure it's dry before you continue working)

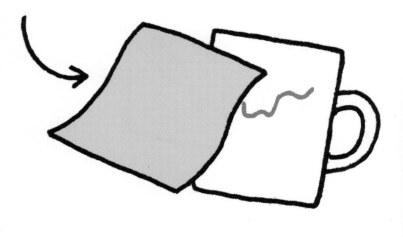

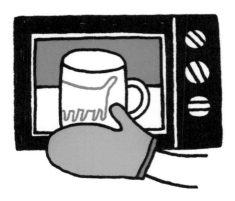

4. If you used paint pens, you can make your mug dishwasher safe by baking it in the oven for 45 minutes at 350*f / 180*c (or whatever your paint pen packaging tells you to do).

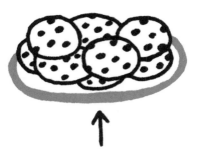

↑

While you wait, eat some cookies. you deserve it.

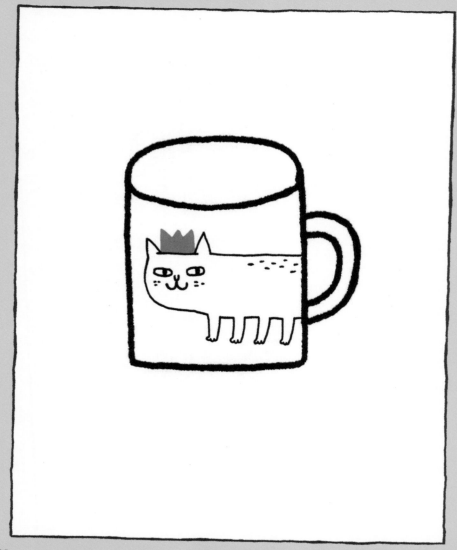

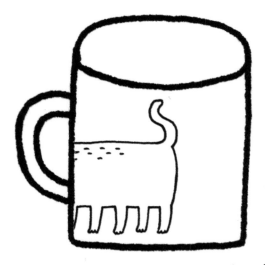

5. Ta da! Let your mug cool, and you're ready to start sipping in style.

About the Illustrator

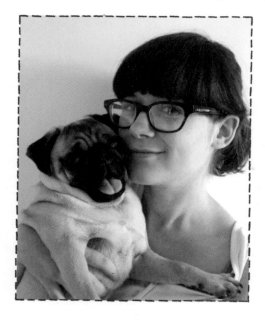

Gemma Correll is a cartoonist, writer, illustrator, and all-around small person. She is the author of *A Cat's Life*, *A Pug's Guide to Etiquette*, and *It's a Punderful Life*, among others. Her illustration clients include Hallmark, *The New York Times*, Oxford University Press, Knock Knock, Chronicle Books, and *The Observer*. Visit www.gemmacorrell.com to see more of Gemma's work.